Juba This
· AND ·
Juba That

SELECTED BY
Virginia Tashjian

ILLUSTRATED BY
Nadine Bernard Westcott

L|B
1837

Little, Brown and Company
Boston New York Toronto London

For My Favorite Storyteller----
My Mother, Zvart Agababian
V.A.T.

For Becky and Wendy
N.B.W.

Compilation copyright © 1969, 1995 by Virginia Tashjian
Illustrations copyright © 1995 by Nadine Bernard Westcott, Inc.

Second Edition

Acknowledgments of permission to reprint previously published material
appear on page 105.

Library of Congress Cataloging-in-Publication Data
Juba this and Juba that / selected by Virginia Tashjian : illustrated by
Nadine Bernard Westcott.—2nd ed.
    p.   cm.
    Includes scores.
    Summary: An anthology of ". . . rhymes and songs to sing and play,
stories to tell and riddles to guess."
    ISBN 0-316-83234-0 (hardcover)
    1. Children's literature. [1. Literature—Collections. 2. Storytelling—
Collections.] I. Tashjian, Virginia A. II. Westcott, Nadine Bernard, ill.
PZ5.T287Ju 1995
820.8'0928—dc20   94-27143

10 9 8 7 6 5 4 3 2

MV-NY

Published simultaneously in Canada
by Little, Brown & Company (Canada) Limited

Printed in the United States of America

Contents

COLLECTOR'S NOTE TO STORYTELLERS

As all storytellers know, there comes a time during the story hour conducted in a library, day care center, or classroom when a change of pace, of tone, and of mood is desirable in order to relax both storyteller and story listener. And, as all parents know, there are often moments with your children (lap-sitting, in the car, at bedtime or mealtime) when a catchy song, story, or rhyme comes in handy.

In order to prevent monotony in the story hour, many storytellers vary the types of stories in any one listening session by including myths, hero tales, or folk stories from various cultures. They may also mix stories with poetry or folk songs or action rhymes.

On the other hand, some storytellers prefer to build their story hours around one theme or mood, and rely on the form rather than the content of their material to provide variety.

In either case, about halfway through the program, a stretch period or break is welcome. During this short five- to ten-minute period, both teller and listener can move tense muscles and relax intensive listening and telling by joining in short verbal exchanges that are fun to do in a group.

The "stretch" does not imply that the children are permitted to leave their seats—for to seat them again into a receptive listening mood may be difficult. The break should consist of stretching vocal muscles or hand and foot movements calculated to provide a change of pace. Baseball's seventh-inning stretch is based on this same sound principle.

The short, simple stories, songs, chants, rhymes, and activities in this book have been used in the "stretch" by this storyteller with maximum success. Many children will enjoy reading the book on their own as well.

CHANTS

• • • •

Chants are a very old form of group entertainment. Don't be afraid to be dramatic, make sure the children follow your actions carefully, and you will have fun playing these chanting games over and over again.

Juba

Juba is an African nickname for a girl born on Monday. This chant originated on plantations in the 1700s as a minstrel show dance done by groups of slaves in which hands, knees, and thighs are clapped and slapped in a rhythmic pattern.

The leader recites the verse first, then the group repeats it several times. The actions are added one at a time:

FIRST TIME: Repeat verse slowly and very loudly in a singsong cadence.

SECOND TIME: Repeat verse a little faster and a little more softly in a singsong cadence. At the same time, clap hands in rhythm.

THIRD TIME: Repeat verse a little faster and even more softly. Slap both hands on knees and then clap hands together in rhythm.

FOURTH TIME: Repeat verse very fast in a very soft voice. At the same time, slap hands on knees, clap hands together, clap hands to both cheeks, then clap hands together again in rhythm.

The leader may repeat the chant as many times as the group wishes, making up more actions.

Juba this and Juba that,
Juba killed a yellow cat.
Juba up and Juba down,
Juba runnin' all around.

Head and Shoulders, Baby

As they recite the first verse of this chant, players touch both hands to their heads, then to their shoulders, then clap on "one, two, three." Other actions are done as suggested in the verses. Still other verses and actions may be added as desired.

Head and shoulders, Baby — one, two, three.
Head and shoulders, Baby — one, two, three.
Head and shoulders, head and shoulders,
Head and shoulders, Baby — one, two, three.

Knee and ankle, Baby — one, two, three.
Knee and ankle, Baby — one, two, three.
Knee and ankle, knee and ankle,
Knee and ankle, Baby — one, two, three.

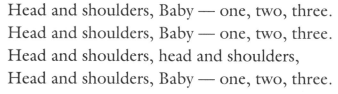

Touch the ground, Baby — one, two, three.
Touch the ground, Baby — one, two, three.
Touch the ground, touch the ground,
Touch the ground, Baby — one, two, three.

Stand up, sit down, Baby — one, two, three.
Stand up, sit down, Baby — one, two, three.
Stand up, sit down, stand up, sit down,
Stand up, sit down, Baby — one, two, three.

— Margaret G. Burroughs

4

Old Hogan's Goat

Although this rhyme may be sung, it is also effective as a chant. The leader chants each line, which is repeated exactly by the children. Everyone claps hands and taps feet in rhythm to the chanting.

Old Hogan's goat
Was feelin' fine;
He ate a red shirt
Right off the line.

I took a stick
And beat his back,
And tied him to
A railroad track.

A speeding train
Was adrawin' nigh;
Old Hogan's goat
Was doomed to die.

He gave an aw-
ful shriek of pain,
Coughed up that shirt,
And flagged that train.

Who Did?

Everyone claps in rhythm as the leader chants the calls in a singsong cadence, the children echo her with the responses, and the leader and group all chime in on the refrains.

CALL: Who did?
RESPONSE: *Who did?*
CALL: Who did?
RESPONSE: *Who did?*
ALL: Who did swallow Jo-Jo-Jo-Jo?

Who did?
Who did?
Who did?
Who did?
ALL: Who did swallow Jo-Jo-Jo-Jo?

Who did?
Who did?
Who did?
Who did?
Who did swallow Jonah?
Who did swallow Jonah?
ALL: Who did swallow Jonah down?

Whale did.
Whale did.
Whale did.
Whale did.

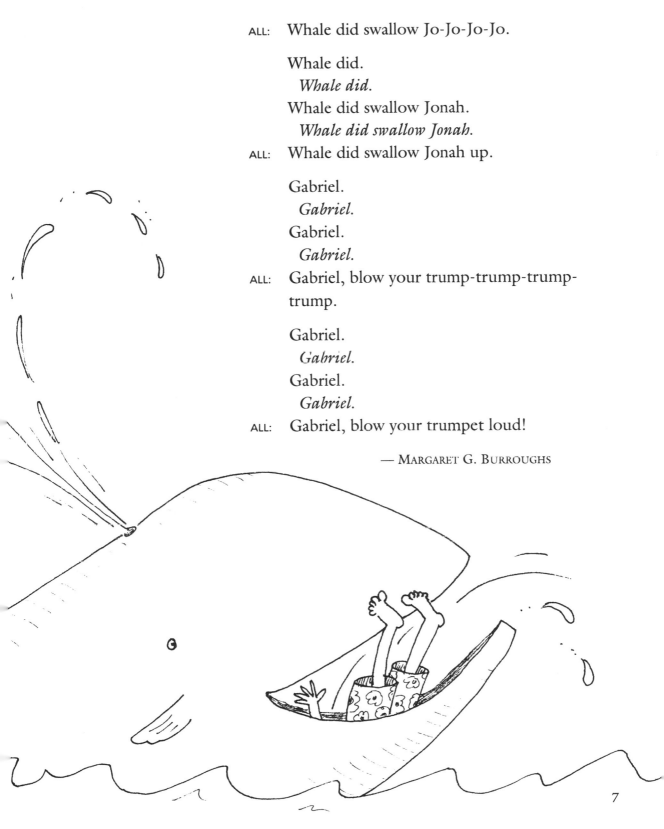

ALL: Whale did swallow Jo-Jo-Jo-Jo.

Whale did.
Whale did.
Whale did swallow Jonah.
Whale did swallow Jonah.

ALL: Whale did swallow Jonah up.

Gabriel.
Gabriel.
Gabriel.
Gabriel.

ALL: Gabriel, blow your trump-trump-trump-trump.

Gabriel.
Gabriel.
Gabriel.
Gabriel.

ALL: Gabriel, blow your trumpet loud!

— MARGARET G. BURROUGHS

The Dark House

The leader chants each line or every half-line in a soft, slow, sepulchral voice. The children repeat each line in the same way. The telling becomes more ghostly and spooky with each line. The last line is spoken by the leader alone and ends in a sudden shout!

In a dark, dark wood, there was a dark, dark house,
And in that dark, dark house, there was a dark, dark room,
And in that dark, dark room, there was a dark, dark cupboard,
And in that dark, dark cupboard, there was a dark, dark shelf,
And in that dark, dark shelf, there was a dark, dark box,
And in that dark, dark box, there was a GHOST!

POEMS AND LIMERICKS

◆ ◆ ◆ ◆

Read these poems at different speeds, allowing the children to guess the subject and finish the rhyme when they can. Then make up some limericks of your own to share with your group.

Seven Little Rabbits

As the leader begins to recite this poem, the repetition will be obvious, and the children will chime in. The leader must begin speaking very slowly so that she can go faster and faster and have enough breath left to finish very fast indeed.

Seven little rabbits
Walkin' down the road
Walkin' down the road
Seven little rabbits
Walkin' down the road
To call on old friend toad.

One little rabbit
Said he was tired
Walkin' down the road
Walkin' down the road
One little rabbit
Said he was tired
Walkin' down the road
To call on old friend toad.

So
Seven little rabbits
Turned around
Until they found
Down in the ground
A hole
Built by a mole.

Seven little rabbits
Went down the hole
Built by the mole
Down in the ground
Until they found
A den.

Then
The seventh little rabbit
Went to sleep —
Now don't say "Peep" —
He's tucked in bed
And now instead

Six little rabbits
Walkin' down the road
Walkin' down the road
Six little rabbits
Walkin' down the road
To call on old friend toad.

One little rabbit
Said he was tired
Walkin' down the road
Walkin' down the road
One little rabbit
Said he was tired
Walkin' down the road
To call on old friend toad.

So
Six little rabbits
Turned around
Until they found
Down in the ground
A hole
Built by a mole.

Six little rabbits
Went down the hole
Built by the mole
Down in the ground
Until they found
A den.

Then
The sixth little rabbit
Went to sleep —
Now don't say "Peep" —
He's tucked in bed
And now instead

Five little rabbits
Walkin' down the road
Walkin' down the road
Five little rabbits
Walkin' down the road
To call on old friend toad.

One little rabbit
Said he was tired
Walkin' down the road
Walkin' down the road
One little rabbit
Said he was tired
Walkin' down the road
To call on old friend toad.

So
Five little rabbits
Turned around
Until they found
Down in the ground
A hole
Built by a mole.

Five little rabbits
Went down the hole
Built by the mole
Down in the ground
Until they found
A den.

Then
The fifth little rabbit
Went to sleep —
Now don't say "Peep" —
He's tucked in bed
And now instead

Four little rabbits
Walkin' down the road
Walkin' down the road
Four little rabbits
Walkin' down the road
To call on old friend toad.

One little rabbit
Said he was tired
Walkin' down the road
Walkin' down the road
One little rabbit
Said he was tired
Walkin' down the road
To call on old friend toad.

So
Four little rabbits
Turned around
Until they found
Down in the ground
A hole
Built by a mole.

Four little rabbits
Went down the hole
Built by the mole
Down in the ground
Until they found
A den.

Then
The fourth little rabbit
Went to sleep —
Now don't say "Peep" —
He's tucked in bed
And now instead

Three little rabbits
Walkin' down the road
Walkin' down the road
Three little rabbits
Walkin' down the road
To call on old friend toad.

One little rabbit
Said he was tired
Walkin' down the road
Walkin' down the road
One little rabbit
Said he was tired
Walkin' down the road
To call on old friend toad.

So
Three little rabbits
Turned around
Until they found
Down in the ground
A hole
Built by a mole.

Three little rabbits
Went down the hole
Built by the mole
Down in the ground
Until they found
A den.

Then
The third little rabbit
Went to sleep —
Now don't say "Peep" —
He's tucked in bed
And now instead

Two little rabbits
Walkin' down the road
Walkin' down the road
Two little rabbits
Walkin' down the road
To call on old friend toad.

One little rabbit
Said he was tired
Walkin' down the road
Walkin' down the road
One little rabbit
Said he was tired
Walkin' down the road
To call on old friend toad.

So
Two little rabbits
Turned around
Until they found
Down in the ground
A hole
Built by a mole.

Two little rabbits
Went down the hole
Built by the mole
Down in the ground
Until they found
A den.

Then
The second little rabbit
Went to sleep —
Now don't say "Peep" —
He's tucked in bed
And now instead

One little rabbit
Walkin' down the road
Walkin' down the road
One little rabbit
Walkin' down the road
To call on old friend toad.

One little rabbit
Said he was tired
Walkin' down the road
Walkin' down the road
One little rabbit
Said he was tired
Walkin' down the road
To call on old friend toad.

So
One little rabbit
Turned around
Until he found
Down in the ground
A hole
Built by a mole.

One little rabbit
Went down the hole
Built by the mole
Down in the ground
Until he found
A den.

Then
The first little rabbit
Who was also the last
Went to sleep —
Now don't say "Peep" —
He's tucked in bed
And now instead
Of walkin' down the road
Of walkin' down the road

The first little rabbit
Dreamed a dream
And to him it seemed
All in a blur
As if there were

Seven little rabbits
Walkin' down the road
Walkin' down the road
Seven little rabbits
Walkin' down the road
To call on old friend toad.

— JOHN BECKER

17

What Did You Put in Your Pocket?

The audience joins in each refrain.

What did you put in your pocket
What did you put in your pocket
  in your pockety pockety pocket
Early Monday morning?

I put in some chocolate pudding
I put in some chocolate pudding
  slushy glushy pudding
Early Monday morning.

REFRAIN: *Slushy glushy pudding!*

What did you put in your pocket
What did you put in your pocket
  in your pockety pockety pocket
Early Tuesday morning?

I put in some ice-cold water
I put in some ice-cold water
  nicy icy water
Early Tuesday morning.

REFRAIN: *Slushy glushy pudding!*
              Nicy icy water!

What did you put in your pocket
What did you put in your pocket
  in your pockety pockety pocket
Early Wednesday morning?

I put in a scoop of ice cream
I put in a scoop of ice cream
  slurpy glurpy ice cream
Early Wednesday morning.

REFRAIN: *Slushy glushy pudding!*
           Nicy icy water!
           Slurpy glurpy ice cream!

What did you put in your pocket
What did you put in your pocket
  in your pockety pockety pocket
Early Thursday morning?

I put in some mashed potatoes
I put in some mashed potatoes
  fluppy gluppy potatoes
Early Thursday morning.

REFRAIN: *Slushy glushy pudding!*
Nicy icy water!
Slurpy glurpy ice cream!
Fluppy gluppy potatoes!

What did you put in your pocket
What did you put in your pocket
  in your pockety pockety pocket
Early Friday morning?

I put in some sticky molasses
I put in some sticky molasses
  sticky icky molasses
Early Friday morning.

REFRAIN: *Slushy glushy pudding!*
Nicy icy water!
Slurpy glurpy ice cream!
Fluppy gluppy potatoes!
Sticky icky molasses!

What did you put in your pocket
What did you put in your pocket
  in your pockety pockety pocket
Early Saturday morning?

21

I put in my five fingers
I put in my five fingers
 funny finny fingers
Early Saturday morning.

REFRAIN: *Slushy glushy pudding!*
           Nicy icy water!
           Slurpy glurpy ice cream!
           Fluppy gluppy potatoes!
           Sticky icky molasses!
           Funny finny fingers!

What did you put in your pocket
What did you put in your pocket
 in your pockety pockety pocket
Early Sunday morning?

I put in a clean white handkerchief
I put in a clean white handkerchief
 a spinky spanky handkerchief
Early Sunday morning.

REFRAIN: *Slushy glushy pudding!*
           Nicy icy water!
           Slurpy glurpy ice cream!
           Fluppy gluppy potatoes!
           Sticky icky molasses!
           Funny finny fingers!
           Spinky spanky handkerchief!

— BEATRICE SCHENK DE REGNIERS

Fire! Fire!

It's fun to make up different rhyming endings for this familiar verse. The leader may omit the last word of each line and let the listeners supply the rhyme.

"Fire! Fire!"
Cried Mrs. _____ (McGuire)

"Where? Where?"
Cried Mrs. _____ (Blair)

"All over town!"
Cried Mrs. _____ (Brown)

"Get some water!"
Cried Mrs. _____ (Potter)

"We'd better jump!"
Cried Mrs. _____ (Gump)

"That would be silly!"
Cried Mrs. _____ (Brunilly)

"It looks too risky!"
Cried Mrs. _____ (Matriski)

"What'll we do?"
Cried Mrs. _____ (La Rue)

"Turn in an alarm!"
Cried Mrs. _____ (La Farme)

"Save us! Save us!"
Cried Mrs. _____ (Potayvus)

The Adventures of Isabel

As the leader recites this poem, the listeners
should chime in on the refrain.

Isabel met an enormous bear,
Isabel, Isabel didn't care;
The bear was hungry, the bear was ravenous,
The bear's mouth was cruel and cavernous.
The bear said, Isabel, glad to meet you,
How do, Isabel, now I'll eat you!
Isabel, Isabel, didn't worry,
Isabel didn't scream or scurry.
She washed her hands and she straightened her hair up,
Then Isabel quietly ate the bear up.

Once in a night as black as pitch
Isabel met a wicked witch.
The witch's face was cross and wrinkled,
The witch's gums with teeth were sprinkled.
Ho, ho, Isabel! the old witch crowed,
I'll turn you into an ugly toad!
Isabel, Isabel, didn't worry,
Isabel didn't scream or scurry.
She showed no rage and she showed no rancor,
But she turned the witch into milk and drank her.

— OGDEN NASH

This Man Had Six Eyes

To make this poem doubly enjoyable, do not
read all of the last line; give the children time to
guess the identity of the "man."

I met a man that had six eyes
And still he could not see.
He lay in bed and hid his head
And would not look at me.

I pulled him up and took him home
(I don't think I did wrong.)
And I let him stay, and day by day
I saw his eyes grow long.

I saw them grow out of his head.
I saw them turn to me.
I saw them grow a foot or so.
And *still* he could not see.

"I think he could see the sun," I said,
So I put him on the sill,
And gave him a drink. But what do you think?
His eyes kept growing still.

They grew as long as I was tall.
They grew like a sleepy tree.
They grew to the floor and out the door.
And still they could not see.

Now what do you think has eyes that long?
You may tell me now if you know.
Or look in the pot: there, like as not,
You will find . . . MR. POT 8 OH!

— JOHN CIARDI

I Know an Old Lady Who Swallowed a Fly

Although this rhyme may also be sung, it is equally effective for a group to recite together. The leader starts, and the children chime in.

I know an old lady who swallowed a fly.
I don't know why she swallowed a fly.
I think she'll die.

I know an old lady who swallowed a spider.
It wiggled and jiggled and tickled inside her.
She swallowed the spider to catch the fly.
I don't know why she swallowed a fly.
I think she'll die.

I know an old lady who swallowed a bird.
How absurd to swallow a bird!
She swallowed the bird to catch the spider,
She swallowed the spider to catch the fly.
I don't know why she swallowed a fly.
I think she'll die.

I know an old lady who swallowed a cat.
Think of that! She swallowed a cat.
She swallowed the cat to catch the bird.
She swallowed the bird to catch the spider.
She swallowed the spider to catch the fly.
I don't know why she swallowed a fly.
I think she'll die.

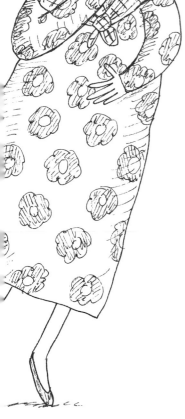

I know an old lady who swallowed a dog.
Oh, what a hog to swallow a dog!
She swallowed the dog to catch the cat,
She swallowed the cat to catch the bird,
She swallowed the bird to catch the spider.
She swallowed the spider to catch the fly,
I don't know why she swallowed a fly.
I think she'll die.

I know an old lady who swallowed a cow.
I don't know how she swallowed a cow.
She swallowed the cow to catch the dog,
She swallowed the dog to catch the cat,
She swallowed the cat to catch the bird,
She swallowed the bird to catch the spider,
She swallowed the spider to catch the fly,
I don't know why she swallowed a fly.
I think she'll die.

I know an old lady who swallowed a horse.
She died, of course!

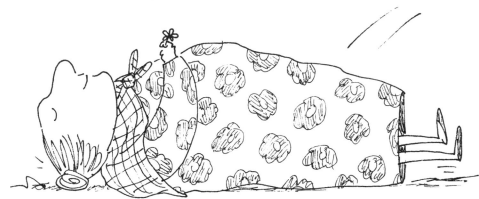

Antonio

Read this poem through once slowly and with exaggerated concern; on the second reading, invite the children to join in — if they don't do so spontaneously.

Antonio, Antonio,
Was tired of living alonio.
   He thought he would woo
   Miss Lissamy Loo
Miss Lissamy Lucy Molonio.

Antonio, Antonio,
Rode off on his polo-polonio.
   He found the fair maid
   In a bowery shade,
A-sitting and knitting alonio.

Antonio, Antonio,
Said, "If you will be my ownio,
    I'll love you true,
    And I'll buy for you,
An icery creamery conio!"

"Oh, NOnio, Antonio! . .
You're far too bleak and bonio!
    And all that I wish,
    You singular fish,
Is that you will quickly begonio."

Antonio, Antonio,
He uttered a dismal moanio;
    Then ran off and hid
    (Or I'm told that he did)
In the Antarctical Zonio.

— LAURA E. RICHARDS

Limericks

There once was a boy of Baghdad,
An inquisitive sort of a lad.
    He said, "I will see
    If a sting has a bee."
And he very soon found that it had!

A flea and a fly in a flue
Were caught, so what could they do:
    Said the fly, "Let us flee."
    "Let us fly," said the flea.
So they flew through a flaw in the flue.

There once was a plesiosaurus
That lived when the earth was all porous.
    But it fainted with shame
    When it first heard its name,
And departed long ages before us.

An oyster from Kalamazoo
Confessed he was feeling quite blue,
    "For," says he, "as a rule,
    When the weather turns cool,
I invariably get in a stew!"

A sleeper from the Amazon
Put nighties of his gra'mazon —
    The reason, that
    He was too fat
To get his own pajamazon.

If You Ever

The leader should recite this rhyme alone once.
When the children recognize the rhythm, they
will chime in.

If you ever ever ever ever ever,
  If you ever ever ever meet a whale,
You must never never never never never,
  You must never never never touch its tail:
For if you ever ever ever ever ever,
  If you ever ever ever touch its tail,
You will never never never never never,
  You will never never meet another whale.

STORIES

♦ ♦ ♦ ♦

These are all audience-participation and action stories of one kind or another. In order to enjoy them fully, encourage listeners to sing out the refrains and repetitions along with you.

Where the story calls for repeated actions, the group should follow the leader carefully. You will discover how much more fun it is when any-one makes a mistake!

The Yellow Ribbon

This story may be expanded or shortened to fit the mood and available time; it's shrinkable or stretchable!

Once there was a boy named John and a girl named Jane. John loved Jane very much. They lived next door to each other, and they went to first grade together, and John did love Jane very much. Every day John would carry Jane's books to school, and every day Jane wore a yellow ribbon around her neck.

One day John said, "Jane, why do you wear that yellow ribbon around your neck?"

"I can't tell," said Jane, "and anyway I don't feel like telling you." But John kept asking, and finally Jane said maybe she'd tell him later sometime.

The next year John and Jane were in the second grade. One day John asked again, "Janey, why do you wear that yellow ribbon around your neck?"

"It's not really your affair, John; maybe I'll tell you sometime . . . but not now," said Jane.

Time went by; John still loved Jane and Jane loved John. And John carried Jane's books to school and Jane wore the yellow ribbon around her neck. They were in the fourth grade . . . then came the sixth grade . . . then junior high school. And every once in a while John asked Jane why she wore the yellow ribbon, but Jane never told. "We've been friends a long time, John. What difference does it make?" she said. And so time went by.

John and Jane went through high school together. John still loved Jane and Jane loved John. John carried Jane's books to school and Jane still wore the yellow ribbon around her neck. On graduation day John said, "Jane, we're graduating now. Won't you *please* tell me why you wear that yellow ribbon around your neck?"

"Oh John," said Jane, "there's no point in telling you on graduation day . . . but someday I will." And that day passed.

Time went by, and John still loved Jane and Jane loved John and Jane still wore that yellow ribbon around her neck.

One day, John and Jane became engaged. John loved Jane and Jane loved John. "Why do you wear that yellow ribbon around your neck, Jane honey?" said John, and finally Jane said maybe she would tell him why on their wedding day.

But the wedding day came and what with all the preparations for the wedding and the honeymoon and all, John just forgot to ask. But several days later, John asked Jane why she wore that yellow ribbon around her neck.

"Well, we are happily married and we love each other, so what difference does it make, John?" said Jane. So John let that pass, but he still *did* want to know.

Time went by. John loved Jane and Jane loved John. Lovely children were born to them, and they were so busy bringing them up that before they knew it, it was their golden wedding anniversary.

"Jane, why do you wear that yellow ribbon around your neck?" asked John once more. And Jane said, "Since you have waited this long, you can wait a little longer. I'll tell you someday, John."

Time went by. John loved Jane and Jane loved John. Finally Jane was taken very ill and was dying. John bent on his knees by her bedside, and with sobs in his voice, asked, "Janey, *please* tell me: Why do you wear that yellow ribbon around your neck?"

"All right, John. You may untie it now," said Jane.

So John did . . . AND JANE'S HEAD FELL OFF!

— Maria Leach

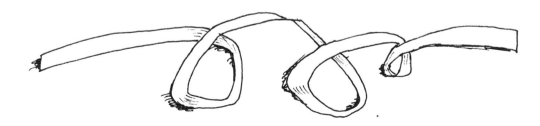

The Snooks Family

An audience-participation story. The leader demonstrates each "huffing and puffing" motion, and the group joins in.

One night, Mr. and Mrs. Snooks were going to bed as usual. It so happened that Mrs. Snooks got into bed first, and she said to her husband, "Please, Mr. Snooks, would you blow the candle out?"

And Mr. Snooks replied, "Certainly, Mrs. Snooks." Whereupon he picked up the candlestick and began to blow, but unfortunately he could only blow by putting his under lip over his upper lip, which meant that his breath went up to the ceiling instead of blowing out the candle flame.

And he puffed and he puffed and he puffed, but he could not blow it out.

So Mrs. Snooks said, "I will do it, my dear," and she got out of bed and took the candlestick from her husband and began to blow. But unfortunately she could only blow by putting her upper lip over her under lip, so that all her breath went down onto the floor. And she puffed and she puffed, but she could not blow the candle out.

So Mrs. Snooks called their son John. John put on his sky-blue dressing gown and slipped his feet into his primrose-colored slippers and came down into his parents' bedroom.

"John, dear," said Mrs. Snooks, "will you please blow out the candle for us?"

And John said, "Certainly, Mummy."

But unfortunately John could only blow out of the right corner of his mouth, so that all his breath hit the wall of the room instead of the candle.

And he puffed and he puffed, but he could not blow out the candle.

So they all called for his sister, little Ann. And little Ann put on her scarlet dressing gown and slipped on her pink slippers and came down to her parents' bedroom.

"Ann, dear," said Mr. Snooks, "will you please blow the candle out for us?"

And Ann said, "Certainly, Daddy."

But unfortunately Ann could only blow out of the left side of her mouth, so that all her breath hit the wall instead of the candle.

And she puffed and she puffed and she puffed, but she could not blow out the candle.

It was just then that they heard in the street below a heavy, steady tread coming along the pavement. Mr. Snooks threw open the window and they all craned their heads out. They saw a policeman coming slowing toward the house.

"Oh, Mr. Policeman," said Mrs. Snooks, "will you come up and blow out our candle? We do so want to go to bed."

"Certainly, Madam," replied the policeman, and he entered and climbed the stairs — *blump, blump, blump*. He came into the bedroom where Mr. Snooks, Mrs. Snooks, John Snooks, and little Ann Snooks were standing around the candle, which they could *not* blow out.

The policeman then picked up the candlestick in a very dignified manner and, putting his mouth into the usual shape for blowing, puffed out the candle at the first puff. Just like this — PUFF!

Then the Snooks family all said, "Thank you, Mr. Policeman."

And the policeman said, "Don't mention it," and turned to go down the stairs again.

"Just a moment, Mr. Policeman," said Mr. Snooks. "You mustn't go down the stairs in the dark. You might fall." And taking a box of matches, he *lit the candle again!*

Mr. Snooks went down the stairs with the policeman and saw him out the door. His footsteps went *blump, blump, blump* along the quiet street.

John Snooks and little Ann Snooks went back to bed. Mr. and Mrs. Snooks got into bed again. There was silence for a moment.

"Mr. Snooks," said Mrs. Snooks, "would you blow out the candle?"

Mr. Snooks got out of bed. "Certainly, Mrs. Snooks," he said. . . . [And so on ad infinitum!]

— Harcourt Williams

The Hobyahs

This story comes from old British folklore. A hobyah is a bogeyman.

Start the first refrain ("Hobyah! Hobyah! Hobyah! Tear down the hemp stalks. Eat up the old man. Eat up the old woman. Carry off the little girl!") in a soft voice. Then the audience should join in, and each successive cry should become louder until the end is very loud and shrill.

Once there was an old man and an old woman and a little girl, and they all lived in a house made of hemp stalks. Now, the old man had a little dog named Turpie; and one night the hobyahs came and said, "*Hobyah! Hobyah! Hobyah! Tear down the hemp stalks. Eat* up the old man. Eat up the old woman. Carry off the little girl!" But little dog Turpie barked so that the hobyahs ran off. And the old man said, "Little dog Turpie barks so that I can neither slumber nor sleep, and if I live till morning, I will cut off his tail."

So in the morning the old man cut off little dog Turpie's tail.

The next night, the hobyahs came again, and said, "Hobyah! Hobyah! Hobyah! Tear down the hemp stalks. Eat up the old man. Eat up the old woman. Carry off the little girl!" But little dog Turpie barked so that the hobyahs ran off; and the old man said, "Little dog Turpie barks so that I can neither slumber nor sleep, and if I live till morning, I will cut off one of his legs."

So in the morning the old man cut off one of little dog Turpie's legs.

The next night, the hobyahs came again and said, "Hobyah! Hobyah! Hobyah! Tear down the hemp stalks. Eat up the old man. Eat up the old woman. Carry off the little girl!" But little dog Turpie barked so that the hobyahs ran off; and the old man said, "Little dog Turpie barks so that I can neither slumber nor sleep, and if I live till morning, I will cut off another of his legs."

So in the morning the old man cut off another of little dog Turpie's legs.

The next night, the hobyahs came again and said, "Hobyah! Hobyah! Hobyah! Tear down the hemp stalks. Eat up the old man. Eat up the old woman. Carry off the little girl!" But little dog Turpie barked so that the hobyahs ran off; and the old man said, "Little dog Turpie barks so that I can neither slumber nor sleep, and if I live till morning, I will cut off another of his legs."

So in the morning the old man cut off another of little dog Turpie's legs.

The next night, the hobyahs came again and said, "Hobyah! Hobyah! Hobyah! Tear down the hemp stalks. Eat up the old man. Eat up the old woman. Carry off the little girl!" But little dog Turpie barked so that the hobyahs ran off; and the old man said, "Little dog Turpie barks so that I can neither slumber nor sleep, and if I live till morning, I will cut off another of his legs."

So in the morning the old man cut off another of little dog Turpie's legs.

The next night, the hobyahs came again and said, "*Hobyah! Hobyah! Hobyah! Tear down the hemp stalks. Eat up the old man. Eat up the old woman. Carry off the little girl!*" But little dog Turpie barked so that the hobyahs ran off; and the old man said, "Little dog Turpie barks so that I can neither slumber nor sleep and if I live till morning, I will cut off little dog Turpie's head!"

So in the morning the old man cut off little dog Turpie's head.

The next night, the hobyahs came again and said, "*Hobyah! Hobyah! Hobyah! Tear down the hemp stalks. Eat up the old man. Eat up the old woman. Carry off the little girl!*" But this time little dog Turpie did not bark, and when the hobyahs found that little dog Turpie's head was off, they tore down the hemp stalks, ate up the old man, ate up the old woman, and carried off the little girl in a bag.

And when the hobyahs came to their home, they hung up the bag with the little girl in it, and every hobyah knocked on the top of the bag and said, "Look me! Look me!" And they went to sleep until the next night, because the hobyahs sleep in the daytime.

The little girl cried a great deal, and a man with a big dog came that way and heard her crying. When he asked her how she came there and she told him, he put the dog in the bag and took the little girl to his home.

The next night the hobyahs took down the bag and knocked on the top of it, and said, "Look me! Look me!" and when they opened the bag . . . the big dog jumped out and ate them all up, every single one.

So-o-o-o — there are no hobyahs left in the world now!

The Busy Farmer's Wife

The leader tells the story and demonstrates the actions. The children imitate the actions. Each motion, once started, is continued after the next one begins so that, by the end of the story, all the motions are going on at once.

The farmer's wife has many duties. She keeps busy all day long. The other day I visited a friend of mine and found her in the kitchen. She was standing at the stove stirring a big pot of apple butter.

(Make stirring motion with right hand.)

The churn was standing nearby and she was pumping the handle up and down as she stirred the apple butter.

(Make pumping motion up and down with left hand; continue stirring motion with the right hand.)

One of the girls came in with a piece of taffy she had made at a taffy party, and put a piece in her mother's mouth. So there my friend stood, stirring and pumping the churn and chewing.

(Make chewing motion with mouth while continuing other motions.)

All of a sudden she noticed that the screen door had been left open and the chickens were coming in the kitchen. She couldn't leave her churning and the apple butter, so all she could do was stand there shaking her head at the chickens and yelling, "Shoo, shoo, shoo."

(Move head up and down as if gesturing
toward the door while making shooing sounds.
Continue all other motions.)

Sody Sallyratus

This story comes from the American South. In pioneer times, baking soda was called saleratus, pronounced "sallyratus."

Be sure to say the "I'll eat you up" lines in unison.

One time there was an old woman and an old man and a little boy and a little girl — and a frisky pet squirrel sittin' up on the fireboard. And one day the old woman wanted to bake some biscuits but she didn't have no sody, so she sent the little boy off to the store for sody sallyratus. The little boy he went trottin' on down the road singin', "Sody, sody, sody, sallyratus!" Trotted across the bridge and on to the store and got the sody sallyratus, and started trottin' on back.

Got to the bridge and started across and an old bear stuck his head out from under it, says:

"I'll eat you up — you and your sody sallyratus!"

So he swallered the little boy — him and his sody sallyratus.

The old woman and the old man and the little girl and the frisky pet squirrel they waited and they waited for the little boy, but he didn't come and didn't come, so finally the old woman sent the little girl after the little boy. She skipped down the road and skipped across the bridge and on to the store, and the storekeeper told her the little boy had already been there and gone. So she started skippin' back, and when she got to the bridge the old bear stuck his head out —

"*I ate a little boy — him and his sody sallyratus — and I'll eat you, too!*"

So he swallered her down.

The old woman and the old man and the frisky pet squirrel, they waited and they waited, but the little girl didn't come and didn't come, so the old woman sent the old man after the little boy and the little girl. He walked on down the road, walked across the bridge — *Karump! Karump! Karump!* — and walked on till he came to the store, and the storekeeper told him the little boy and the little girl had already been there and gone.

"They must'a stopped somewhere 'side the road to play."

So the old man, he started walkin' on back. Got to the bridge —

"*I ate a little boy, him and his sody sallyratus, and I ate a little girl — and I'll eat you, too!*"

And the old bear reached out and grabbed the old man and swallered him.

Well, the old woman and the frisky pet squirrel they waited and waited but the old man didn't come and didn't come. So the old woman, *she* set out a-hunchety-hunchin' down the road, crossed the bridge, got to the store, and the storekeeper told her, says, "That boy's already done been here and gone — him and the little girl and the old man, too."

So the old woman she went hunchin' on back — *a-hunchety-hunchety-hunch*. Got to the bridge —

"*I ate a little boy, him and his sody sallyratus, and I ate a little girl, and I ate an old man — and I'll eat you, too!*"

Reached out and grabbed her, and swallered *her* up.

Well, the frisky pet squirrel, he waited and he waited and he waited, and he went to runnin' back and forth up there on the fireboard, and he was gettin' hungrier and hungrier; so finally he jumped down on the table, jumped onto the bench, and jumped to the floor. Shook his tail out behind him and out the door and down the road, just a-friskin'. Scuttered across the bridge and on into the store. R'ared up on his hindquarters and looked for the storekeeper, squarked a time or two, and when the storekeeper looked up and saw him, the pet squirrel raised up on his tiptoes and asked him had he seen anything of the little boy or the little girl or the old man or the old woman.

"Law, yes! They all done already been here and gone. Surely they ain't *all* done stopped 'side the road to play."

So the pet squirrel he stretched his tail out behind him and frisked out the door. Frisked on over the bridge —

"*I ate a little boy, him and his sody sallyratus, and I ate a little girl, and I ate an old man, and I ate an old woman — and I'll eat you, too!*"

The little frisky pet squirrel, he stuck his tail straight up in the air and just chittered, but by the time the old bear made for him he was already scratchin' halfway up a tree. The old bear he went clamberin' up to get him. The squirrel got 'way out on a limb, and the old bear started out the limb after him. The squirrel he jumped and caught in the next tree.

"*Humpf! If you can make it with your little legs, I KNOW I can make it with my big 'uns!*"

And the old bear tried to jump — didn't quite make it. Down he went and when he hit the ground he split wide open.

The old woman stepped out, and the old man he stepped out, and the little girl jumped, and the little boy he jumped out. And the old woman says, "Where's my sody sallyratus?"

"Here," says the little boy, and he handed it to her.

So they went on back to the house and the frisky pet squirrel he scooted on ahead of 'em, cloomb back up on the fireboard, and curled his tail over his back, and watched the old woman till she took the biscuits out the oven. So then she broke him off a chunk and blew on it till it wasn't too hot, and handed it up to him. And he took it in his forepaws and turned it over and over and nibbled on it — and when he ate it up he leaned down and chittered for some more. And he was so hungry the old woman had to hand him chunks till he'd eaten two whole biscuits.

— RICHARD CHASE

THE LION HUNT

Lion hunting is dangerous, so it's important to stay together. The group must repeat everything exactly as the leader says it and does it.

LEADER: Do you want to go on a lion hunt?
(Children may answer in various ways. The leader reminds them that they must repeat her words and actions exactly.)

GROUP: *Do you want to go on a lion hunt?*
LEADER: Well, then, let's go.
GROUP: *Well, then, let's go.*

This pattern of repeating every line and action continues throughout the whole story.

Let's start walking.

> (Make walking sounds with feet on floor.)

We'll have to cross a bridge.

> (Hit palms on thighs to simulate sound of feet on
> bridge.)

Now we're across the bridge.
Horses are waiting for us here.
We'll ride part of the way.

> (Hold reins in hands. Bounce up and down. Make cluck-
> ing sounds with tongue to simulate sound of horses'
> hooves on ground. Give occasional "giddy-up.")

This is as far as we can go with the horses.
We'll have to walk from here.

> (Make walking sounds with feet.)

Oh! It's beginning to rain.

> (Rub palms together in circular motion to make sound
> of rain.)

It's getting muddy.
We'll have to walk in the mud.
It's hard going.

> (Make claws of hands, turn palms down, and make
> motions in walking rhythm as if pulling feet in mud.
> Make juicy, slurpy sounds with mouth.)

In fact, we're walking through a bog.
>(Continue slurping sound and same motions.)

The mosquitoes are biting.
>(Slap at face and neck; scratch here and there; continue slurping walk through bog.)

We're finally on dry ground now.
We can walk a little faster.
>(Make walking sounds with feet.)

Uh-oh, wait a minute.
I think I see something.
>(Hold hand to eye.)

Yes, I see a stream.
Shall we take a run?
And jump over it?
Ready?
Let's go.

>(Make running rhythm, slapping palms on thighs. Raise palms in midair, hold for a moment, then hit thigh again, simulating sounds of a jump over the stream.)

We made it!

We'll have to walk through the reeds.

> (Put hands in front of face to separate reeds that block passage.)

Now we're on clear ground again.

> (Make walking sounds with hands slapping thighs.)

Stop!

Wait a minute.

I see a big river.

Let's take a long run.

And a big jump.

If we don't make it, we'll have to swim.

Ready?

Run!

> (Make running rhythm, slapping palms on thighs. Raise hands and hold in midair for a moment.)

We'll never make it.

We'll have to swim.

> (Hold nose with hands as if diving into water. Make spluttering noises. Begin swimming strokes.)

We can walk the rest of the way.

> (Make slurping sounds; pretend to walk in slow, painful crawl.)

Well, we made it to shore.

>   (Wring out clothes
>   and hair and shake self.)

It ought to be easier from here on.
Let's go.

>   (Make walking rhythm with feet.)

Hold it.

>   (Put hand to eyes.)

I see a cave.
Shall we go in?
Careful now, here we go.

>   (Cup hands to mouth
>   once inside cave.)

It's dark in here.
I wonder if there's anyone here.
Yoo-hoo.

>   (Louder.)

I hear an echo.
Yooooooo-hooooooo.

Hey.

I just happened to think of something.

There may be bears in here.

Let's get out of here.

> **(Make running sounds with feet.)**

Phew!

I'm glad we got out of there safely.

We'll have to climb this hill.

> **(Make slow walking rhythm.)**

It's getting steeper and steeper.

We'll have . . . to . . . go . . . slower . . . and slower.

Phew!

We're almost to the top.

Just a little farther.

> **(Make footsteps slower and slower.)**

Now we're at the top.

Let's rest a minute.

Take a deep breath.

> **(Take a loud sniff.)**

Isn't the air wonderful?

> **(Hit hands on chest.)**

Makes you feel so good.

Look at the beautiful view.

(Put hands to eyes, turning complete
circle as though looking around.)

Everybody rested?
Shall we run down the hill?
Ready?
Get set.
Go!

(Make running rhythm with
feet on floor.)

Shhhhhhhhhhhhhhh.

(Put finger to mouth.)

We're near lion country.
We'll walk through this tall grass.
Grass makes a swishing sound.

(Slap palms together in swishing, not clapping sound.
Make swishing sound with mouth.)

Stop.

(In whisper.)

This is where I last saw a lion.
Let's climb a tree.

(Curve arms as if climbing tree.
Move hands higher and higher.)

Careful, don't fall, now.

Hold on tight.
Let's look in this direction.
See anything?
I don't see anything.
Let's look in this direction.

> (Hold tree with one hand;
> put other hand to eye.)

See anything?
I don't see anything.
Look over here.
Can you see anything?
I don't see anything.
Now look this way.
Shuuuuuuuuuuush!
I think I see something.
It has two big eyes.
And a long tail.
It's waving back and forth.
Back and forth.
It looks like a lion.
It IS a lion.

Let's get out of here.

> (Make motion of sliding down the tree. Whole party retraces steps in a dash, running up the hill, down the hill, and into the cave.)

Let's wait here.
The lion may not find us.
Shhhhhhhh.
Now, carefully, let's tiptoe out.

> (Make motion of tiptoe walking.)

Now hurry!

> (Retrace route in double-quick time, swimming the river, walking over hard ground, walking through the reeds, running and jumping the stream, walking over the dry ground, walking through the bog, walking in the mud, walking through the rain sounds, riding horses, walking over the bridge, and so on.)

We made it.
Phew! That was close!

The Shopping Trip

The leader tells the story and accompanies it with motions. The audience mimics the motions. Each motion, once started, is continued after the next one begins so that before the end of the story, hands, feet, head, and jaws are all in motion.

We're all going on a shopping trip in the big department store.
(Name a local one.)

We're going to buy a pair of scissors first.
(Make a cutting motion with forefinger and middle finger of right hand.)

We need a new set of steps for the back porch.
(Make walking-up-steps motion with feet.)

There was a sale of rocking chairs, so we bought one.
(Add a rocking motion back and forth in chair
while walking with feet and cutting with fingers.)

We got thirsty walking around and put a big piece of bubble gum in our mouths.
(Make lump in cheek with tongue, and begin chewing.)

At this moment, our heads began to itch.
(Scratch head and remember to continue all motions.)

The salesman came up to us and asked if we wanted to buy anything else, and we all said no.
(Shake head from side to side and continue all motions.)

I Went to the Library

Storytellers often make up their own special games for the stretch period. In this one, each player in turn has a chance to name a book title, but he or she must repeat all the previously named titles to stay in the game. Those who cannot remember all previous titles are out; the last player left wins the game. If the group is too large, a few at a time may be chosen to play.

LEADER: I went to the library, and I read *Tom Sawyer.*

> (Any title may be chosen.)

FIRST PLAYER: I went to the library, and I read *Tom Sawyer* and *Curious George.*

> (Another title is added.)

SECOND PLAYER: I went to the library, and I read *Tom Sawyer, Curious George,* and *The Cat in the Hat.*

> (A third title is added.)

THIRD PLAYER: I went to the library, and I read *Tom Sawyer, Curious George, The Cat in the Hat,* and *Charlotte's Web.*

And so on.

ACTION RHYMES

• • • •

Action rhymes are fun to do either one on one or in groups. Directions are provided here, but you can also make up your own verses and gestures.

CLAP YOUR HANDS

Carry out the actions indicated by the rhyme. Other actions may be added at the suggestion of the children, such as "wiggle your ears," "touch your nose," or "make a fist."

Clap your hands, clap your hands;
Clap them just like me.

Touch your shoulders, touch your shoulders;
Touch them just like me.

Tap your knees, tap your knees;
Tap them just like me.

Shake your head, shake your head;
Shake it just like me.

Clap your hands, clap your hands;
Now let them quiet be.

Miss Polly Had a Dolly

Miss Polly had a dolly
Who was sick, sick, sick,
> (Crook your arms as if holding a baby,
> and make a rocking motion.)

So she phoned for the doctor
To come quick, quick, quick.
> (Pantomime making a phone call.)

The doctor came
With his bag and hat,
> (Swing one arm as if holding a briefcase.)

And he knocked on the door
With a *rat-tat-tat*.
> (Knock on the floor.)

He looked at the dolly,
And he shook his head;
> (Shake head.)

Then he said, "Miss Polly,
Put her straight to bed."
> (Shake finger.)

He wrote on a paper
For a pill, pill, pill;
> ("Write" on palm.)

"I'll be back in the morning
With my bill, bill, bill."
> (Wave good-bye.)

Hands on Shoulders

Carry out the actions indicated by the rhyme.

Hands on shoulders, hands on knees,
Hands behind you, if you please;
Touch your shoulders, now your nose,
Now your hair, and now your toes;
Hands up high in the air,
Down at your sides and touch your hair;
Hands up high as before,
Now clap your hands, one, two, three, four.

HANDS UP

Carry out the actions indicated by the rhyme.

Reach for the ceiling,
Touch the floor;
Stand up again;
Let's do more.

Touch your head,
Then your knee;
Up to your shoulder,
Like this — see?

Reach for the ceiling,
Touch the floor.
That's all now —
There isn't any more.

My Eyes Can See

My eyes can see.
> (Make "eyeglasses" with hands.)

My mouth can talk.
> (Move thumb and index finger as if talking.)

My ears can hear.
> (Cup hand, and place it behind ear.)

My feet can walk.
> (Make second and third fingers of right hand "walk.")

My nose can smell.
> (Touch nose.)

My teeth can bite.
> (Move thumb and fingers together and apart as if chewing.)

My eyelids can flutter.
> (Hold hands up to eyes and flutter fingers.)

My hands can write.
> (Pretend to hold pen and write.)

But when the clock
Its time does show,
I'll take some books
> (Pantomime picking up some books.)

And away I'll go.
> (Wave good-bye.)

The Teapot

I'm a little teapot, short and stout.
This is my handle,

　　　(Put one hand on hip.)

This is my spout.

　　　(Extend opposite hand outward and slant it down for
　　　spout.)

When I get all steamed up and shout,
Just tip me over and pour me out.

　　　(Bend body toward arm extended as spout.)

The Turtle

There was a little turtle.
He lived in a box.

> (Put index finger of right hand in upward palm of left hand.)

He swam in a puddle.

> (Make circular motion as if in a puddle.)

He climbed on the rocks.

> (Climb over the fingertips for "rocks.")

He snapped at a mosquito;

> (Make snapping motion by raising and lowering fingers and thumb of right hand.)

He snapped at a flea;
He snapped at a minnow;
He snapped at me.

He caught the mosquito.

> (Clasp and unclasp as if catching something.)

He caught the flea;
He caught the minnow;
But he didn't catch me.

> (Point to self.)

Eensy-Weensy Spider

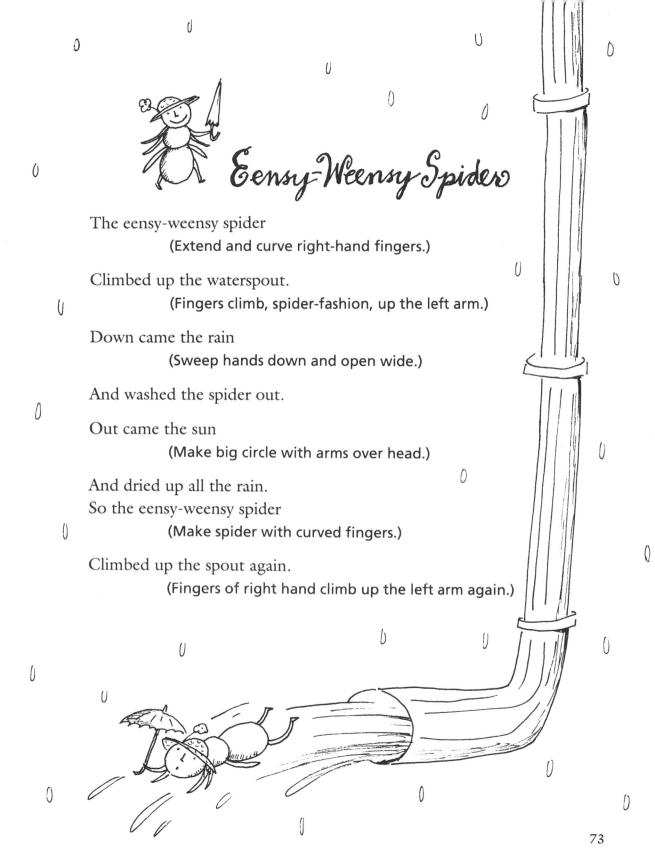

The eensy-weensy spider
  (Extend and curve right-hand fingers.)

Climbed up the waterspout.
    (Fingers climb, spider-fashion, up the left arm.)

Down came the rain
    (Sweep hands down and open wide.)

And washed the spider out.

Out came the sun
    (Make big circle with arms over head.)

And dried up all the rain.
So the eensy-weensy spider
    (Make spider with curved fingers.)

Climbed up the spout again.
    (Fingers of right hand climb up the left arm again.)

Five Little Fishies

Five little fishies
Swimming in the pool.

> (Make swimming motions.)

The first one said,
"This pool is cool."

> (Hug yourself as if you're freezing.)

The second one said,
"This pool is deep."

> (Point down.)

The third one said,
"I'd like to sleep."

> (Close eyes, and rest head on hand "pillow.")

The fourth one said,
"Let's swim and dip."

> (Make swimming and diving motions.)

The fifth one said,
"I see a ship."

> (Look out to "sea.")

The fisherman's line went
Splish, splish, splash,

> (Flutter fingers.)

(Fast:) And away the five

Little fishies dash!

> (Put hands behind back.)

RIDDLES

◆ ◆ ◆

Some of the riddles here are like puzzles; you must guess the answers. Others have trick endings. You may have your own favorites that you will want to share with your group.

Pete and Repeat

Continue to repeat this riddle louder and louder and more impatiently until the group dissolves in laughter.

LEADER: Pete and Repeat were walking down the street. Suddenly Pete went away. Who was left?

GROUP: *Repeat.*

(Louder:)

LEADER: Pete and Repeat were walking down the street. Suddenly Pete went away. Who was left?

GROUP: *Repeat.*

(Very loud:)

LEADER: Pete and Repeat were walking . . . [etc.]

'Arry 'Arrington

The leader continues to repeat this riddle until the group stops giving the responses of its own accord.

LEADER: 'E was the greatest man on earth.
GROUP: *Who was?*
LEADER: 'E was.
GROUP: *Who was 'e?*
LEADER: 'Arry 'Arrington.
GROUP: *Who was 'Arry 'Arrington?*
LEADER: 'E was the greatest man on earth.
GROUP: *Who was?*

Transportation Problem

Once there was a man who was set the task of taking a wolf, a goat, and a cabbage across the river. When he came to the river, he found that the boat was so small it would hold one man and only *one other* thing.

What was he to do? How could he take the wolf, the goat, and the cabbage over, one at a time, so that the wolf wouldn't eat the goat and the goat wouldn't eat the cabbage?

ANSWER:

1. Take the goat over, then come back.
2. Take the wolf over and take the goat back.
3. Take the cabbage over (leaving the goat behind).
4. Go back and get the goat.

OR

1. Take the goat over, then come back.
2. Take the cabbage over and take the goat back.
3. Take the wolf over (leaving the goat behind).
4. Go back and get the goat.

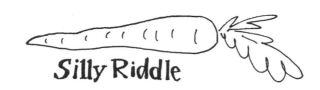

Silly Riddle

Once there was a donkey in a field. On one side of the field stood a ten-foot wall. On the other side, a wide, deep river flowed, and along the third side ran a thick prickly hedge. On the fourth side, a steep high cliff rose. In a field close by, there was a heap of carrots. How did the donkey get to the carrots?

The group's guesses and the leader's responses will go something like this, until the correct answer is finally given:

GROUP: *Jump over the wall?*

LEADER: No, it was too high.

GROUP: *Swim the river?*

LEADER: No, he couldn't swim.

GROUP: *Push through the hedge?*

LEADER: No, it was too thick and prickly.

GROUP: *Climb the cliff?*

LEADER: No, it was too steep.

GROUP: (Correct answer): *Well, we don't know.*

LEADER: Neither did the donkey!

RHYMING RIDDLES

Riddle 1

What would happen very soon
If you swallowed your cereal spoon?

Riddle 2

Riddle me, riddle me, riddle me reet;
When do elephants have eight feet?

Riddle 3

What can you see
Down in the lake
That's always free
But that no one can take?

Riddle 4

What do the children
In China call
Young yellow cats
When they are small?

81

The Toaster

For full enjoyment of this riddle, do not reveal
the title; read the poem and ask for guesses as
to what it's about.

A silver-scaled Dragon with jaws flaming red
Sits at my elbow and toasts my bread.
I hand him fat slices, and then, one by one,
He hands them back when he sees they are done.

— WILLIAM JAY SMITH

SONGS

◆ ◆ ◆ ◆

Here are some songs that you will enjoy singing
and acting out. For more fun, you can make up
your own words and actions for many of them.

Smoke Goes up the Chimney

This song may be sung on one note or to a made-up tune.

1. First sing the song through with all the motions.

2. Next repeat it, being quiet on "push the damper in" but making the motion in rhythm.

3. The third time through, be quiet on "push the damper in" and "pull the damper out" but make the motions in rhythm.

4. Repeat, being quiet on "push the damper in," "pull the damper out," and the first "smoke goes up the chimney" but making the motions in rhythm.

5. Repeat and be quiet on all lines, but make the motions in rhythm. The last time you sing, the only words will be:

Oh, you (*motion*)

And you (*motion*)

And the (*motion*)

(*motion*) (*motion*)

And the (*motion*)

Oh, you push the damper in,
>(Push right arm forward.)

And you pull the damper out,
>(Pull arm back.)

And the smoke goes up the chimney
>(Make spiral motion.)

Just the same, just the same,
>(Wave right arm to side; wave left arm to side.)

And the smoke goes up the chimney just the same.
>(Repeat spiral motion.)

IF YOU'RE HAPPY AND YOU KNOW IT

Have everyone join in doing the actions mentioned. Add your own verses, which might include all kinds of actions, such as stamping your feet, wiggling your ears, touching your toes, or crossing your legs.

If you're hap-py and you know it, clap your hands, *(Clap, clap)* If you're

hap-py and you know it, clap your hands, _ If you're *(Clap, clap)* hap-py and you know it, then the

whole wide world should know it, If you're hap-py and you know it, clap your hands. *(Clap, clap)*

BINGO

1. First the leader sings the whole song straight through.

2. The whole group repeats the song but keeps silent on the letter *B,* clapping hands in rhythm instead.

3. Repeat the song but keep silent on the letters *B* and *I,* clapping hands in rhythm instead.

4. Continue to repeat the song, keeping silent on each successive letter. The final and sixth time will have five claps instead of singing "*B-I-N-G-O.*"

There was a farm-er had a dog, And Bin-go was his name-oh. B - I - N - G - O,

B - I - N - G - O, B - I - N - G - O, Bin-go was his name - oh.

2. That farmer's dog at our back door,
   Begging for a bone, -oh.
   B-I-N-G-O, B-I-N-G-O
   B-I-N-G-O,
   Bingo was his name, -oh.

Today Is Monday

You may want to make up your own menu after
the first verse.

To - day is Mon - day, to - day is Mon - day.

Mon - day, string beans; All you hun - gry chil - dren, Come and eat it up.

2. Today is Tuesday, today is Tuesday.
Tuesday, spaghetti,
Monday, string beans;
All you hungry children,
Come and eat it up.

3. Today is Wednesday, today is Wednesday.
Wednesday, ZOOOOP!
Tuesday, spaghetti,
Monday, string beans;
All you hungry children
Come and eat it up.

4. Today is Thursday, today is Thursday.
Thursday, roast beef . . .
          (Continue as in third verse.)

5. Today is Friday, today is Friday.
Friday, fresh fish . . .
          (Continue as in fourth verse.)

6. Today is Saturday, today is Saturday.
Saturday, chicken . . .
          (Continue as in fifth verse.)

7. Today is Sunday, today is Sunday.
Sunday, ice cream . . .
          (Continue as in sixth verse.)

John Jacob Jingleheimer Schmidt

Repeat this song as many times as you like, each
time more and more softly. On the last round,
the words are mouthed silently until the last
line, which is shouted as loudly as possible.

John   Ja - cob   Jin - gle - hei - mer Schmidt!   His name ___ is   my   name,

too; _____   When - ev - er   we   go   out,   Hear the   hap - py   peo - ple   shout,

Last time only

"John   Ja - cob Jin - gle - hei - mer   Schmidt, Ta - ra - ra - ra - ra - ra - ra - ra!"

Put Your Finger in the Air

As you sing, act out the motions described.

Put your fin-ger in the air, in the air; Put your fin-ger in the air, in the air, Put your

fin-ger in the air. Tell me, how's the air up there? Put your fin-ger in the air, _ in the air.

2. Put your finger on your head, on your head;
Put your finger on your head, on your head.
Put your finger on your head. Tell me, is it green or red?
Put your finger on your head, on your head.

3. Put your finger on your cheek, on your cheek;
Put your finger on your cheek, on your cheek.
Put your finger on your cheek. Leave it there a week.
Put your finger on your cheek, on your cheek.

4. Put your finger on your nose, on your nose;
Put your finger on your nose, on your nose.
Put your finger on your nose. Is that where the cold wind blows?
Put your finger on your nose, on your nose.

5. Put your finger on your chest, on your chest;
Put your finger on your chest, on your chest.
Put your finger on your chest. Give it just a little rest.
Put your finger on your chest, on your chest.

6. Put your finger on your belly, on your belly;
Put your finger on your belly, on your belly.
Put your finger on your belly. Make it shake like apply jelly.
Put your finger on your belly, on your belly.

— WOODY GUTHRIE

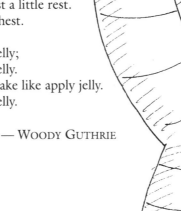

I Wish I Was a Mole in the Ground

Begin by singing a few verses of this song. Then ask individual children to make wishes. Make up a rhyme on the spur of the moment, and continue the song. Verses three through five shown here are some examples made up by children in a library story hour.

I wish I was a mole in the ground, I wish I was a mole in the ground. If I was a

mole in the ground, I'd _ root that moun-tain down, _ And I wish I was a mole in the ground.

2. I wish I was a lizard in the spring,
   I wish I was a lizard in the spring.
   If I was a lizard in the spring,
   I'd hear my sweetheart sing.
   And I wish I was a lizard in the spring.

3. I wish I was a horse in the stable,
   I wish I was a horse in the stable.
   If I was a horse in the stable,
   I'd canter when I was able.
   And I wish I was a horse in the stable.

4. I wish I was an ant in the grass,
   I wish I was an ant in the grass.
   If I was an ant in the grass,
   I'd tickle a little lass.
   And I wish I was an ant in the grass.

5. I wish I was a bird in a tree,
   I wish I was a bird in a tree.
   If I was a bird in a tree,
   I'd see what I could see.
   And I wish I was a bird in a tree.

My Bonnie Lies over the Ocean

1. Sing the whole song through the first time with no motions.

2. Repeat the whole song a second time demonstrating the following motions:

"my" — Point to self.

"bonnie" — Make figure of a girl in the air with both hands.

"lies" — Put hands together and make a circle with the arms to indicate a cradle or bed.

"over" — Point faraway.

"ocean" — Make wavy motion with the right hand.

"sea" — Make wavy motion with right hand, but with a choppy, sharper stroke to differentiate from "ocean."

"oh" — Join thumbs and index fingers in round O.

"bring" — Make beckoning motion with the right hand.

"back" — Touch back of left shoulder with right hand.

"to" — Hold up two fingers.

"me" — Point to self again.

3. Go through the motions slowly with the group once or twice; then try the whole song.

My bon-nie lies o-ver the o-cean, — My bon-nie lies o-ver the sea, — My bon-nie lies

o-ver the o-cean, — Oh, bring back my bon-nie to me. — Bring back, bring back, Oh,

bring back my bon-nie to me, — Bring back, bring back, Oh, bring back my bon-nie to me. —

Five Speckled Frogs

This song is especially fun to sing if you insert the names of different children in the blanks. (Or you can just say "one.")

Five lit - tle speck - led frogs Sit - ting on a speck - led log,

Eat - ing the most de - li - cious flies. Yum, yum. *(Child's name)* fell in - to the pool

Where it was so nice and cool; Now there are four green speck-led frogs. Ribbet, ribbet.

2. Four little speckled frogs
   Sitting on a speckled log,
   Eating the most delicious flies.
   Yum, yum.
   _____ fell into the pool
   Where it was so nice and cool;
   Now there are three green speckled frogs.
   Ribbet, ribbet.

96

3. Three little speckled frogs
   Sitting on a speckled log,
   Eating the most delicious flies.
   Yum, yum.
   _____ fell into the pool
   Where it was so nice and cool;
   Now there are two green speckled frogs.
   Ribbet, ribbet.

4. Two little speckled frogs
   Sitting on a speckled log,
   Eating the most delicious flies.
   Yum, yum.
   _____ fell into the pool
   Where it was so nice and cool;
   Now there is one green speckled frog.
   Ribbet, ribbet.

5. One little speckled frog
   Sitting on a speckled log,
   Eating the most delicious flies.
   Yum, yum.
   _____ fell into the pool
   Where it was so nice and cool;
   Now there are no green speckled frogs.
   Ribbet, ribbet.

ONE FINGER KEEP MOVING

One fin - ger keep mov - ing, _____ One fin - ger keep mov - ing, ___

_ One fin - ger keep mov - ing, And we'll all be hap - py and gay. ___

2. One finger,
   (Hold up right index finger.)

Two fingers
   (Hold up left index finger.)

Keep moving.
   (Wiggle both index fingers.)

One finger,
   (Stop wiggling fingers; hold up right index finger.)

Two fingers
   (Show left index finger.)

Keep moving.
   (Wiggle both fingers while singing.)

One finger, two fingers keep moving,
   (Show right, then left forefingers and keep both wiggling.)

And we'll all be happy and gay.
   (Wiggle both fingers.)

3. One finger, two fingers, one thumb, two thumbs keep moving, *etc.*

    (Continue the song by showing each part of the body mentioned and adding one portion at a time as the words dictate; during the singing of "And we'll all be happy and gay," all the accumulated motions must be kept going.)

4. One finger, two fingers, one thumb, two thumbs, one arm, two arms keep moving, *etc.*

5. One finger, two fingers, one thumb, two thumbs, one arm, two arms, one foot, two feet, *etc.*

6. One finger, two fingers, one thumb, two thumbs, one arm, two arms, one foot, two feet, one head (*nod head*), keep moving, *etc.*

7. One finger, two fingers, one thumb, two thumbs, one arm, two arms, one foot, two feet, one head, stand up, sit down, keep moving, *etc.*

John Brown's Baby

John __ Brown's ba - by had a cold up-on his chest,

John _ Brown's _ ba - by had a cold up-on his chest,　　John _ Brown's _ ba - by had a

cold up-on his chest,　And they rubbed him down with cam-phor-at-ed oil.

1. Sing the whole song through the first time with no motions.

2. Repeat the whole song a second time, but remain silent on the word "baby." Instead, crook arms as if holding a baby, and make a baby-rocking motion each time the word "baby" occurs.

3. Repeat the song again, remaining silent on the words "baby" and "cold." Repeat the cradling motion on the word "baby," and make a loud coughing sound in place of the word "cold."

4. Repeat the song again, remaining silent on the words "baby," "cold," and "chest." Substitute the cradling motion for "baby," the loud cough for "cold," and a tap on the chest with the right hand for the word "chest."

5. Repeat the whole song once more, remaining silent on "baby," "cold," "chest," and "rubbed." Repeat the motions already described, and add a rubbing motion on the stomach for "rubbed."

TEN
TONGUE TWISTERS

◆ ◆ ◆ ◆

Many children have enjoyed the tongue twisters included here. Say them as fast as you can as many times as you can, trying not to trip up your tongue!

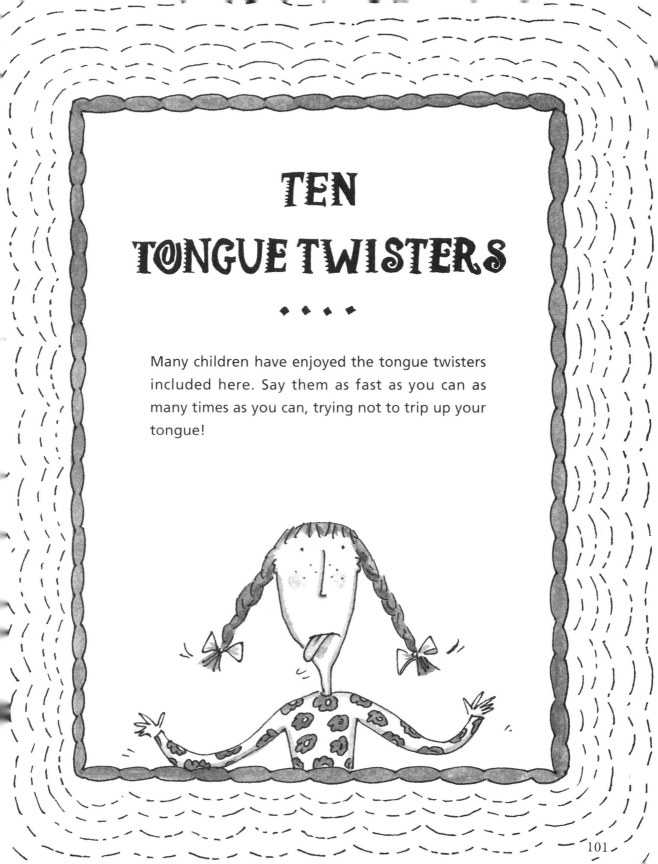

Betty Botter bought some butter, but she said, "This butter is bitter," so she bought a bit of butter better than the bitter butter.

The rat ran over the ridge of the roof with a raw lump of liver in his mouth.

Famous Floyd Fudd Flingle flipped floppy, flat flapjacks.

A big black bug bit a big black bear and made the big black bear bleed blood.

Sally Simpson sold the seashells Sandy saw sitting on the seashore.

Peter Piper picked a peck of pickled peppers.

A skunk sat on a stump — the skunk thought the stump stunk, the stump thought the skunk stunk.

A tutor who tooted the flute tried to tutor a tooter to toot.

Six long slim slick sycamore saplings.

June Julie Jackson joyfully juggled the juicy, wobbly, wiggly, jiggly Jell-o.

Index of Titles

Acknowledgments

John Becker: "Seven Little Rabbits" from *New Feathers for an Old Goose,* by John Becker. Copyright © 1956 by John Becker. Reprinted by permission of Pantheon Books, a division of Random House, Inc. and Routledge & Kegan Paul Ltd.

Sara and John E. Brewton: Five limericks from *Laughable Limericks,* by Sara and John E. Brewton. Text copyright © 1965 by Sara and John E. Brewton. Reprinted by permission of Betty Blackburn.

Margaret G. Burroughs: "Head and Shoulders, Baby" and "Who Did?" from *Did You Feed My Cow?,* published by Thomas Y. Crowell Company in 1956. Reprinted by permission of the author.

Bernice Wells Carlson: "Smoke Goes up the Chimney" from *Act It Out,* by Bernice Wells Carlson. Copyright © 1956 by Abingdon Press. Copyright renewed © 1984 by Bernice Wells Carlson. Reprinted by permission of the author.

Richard Chase: "Sody Sallyratus" from *The Grandfather Tales,* by Richard Chase. Copyright 1948, © renewed 1976 by Richard Chase. Reprinted by permission of Houghton Mifflin Company.

John Ciardi: "This Man Had Six Eyes" from *I Met a Man,* by John Ciardi. Copyright © 1961 by John Ciardi. Reprinted by permission of Houghton Mifflin Company. All rights reserved.

Beatrice Schenk de Regniers: "What Did You Put in Your Pocket?" from *Something Special,* by Beatrice Schenk de Regniers. Copyright © 1958 by Beatrice Schenk de Regniers. Copyright © renewed 1986 by Beatrice Schenk de Regniers. Reprinted by permission of Marian Reiner for the author.

Marian Grayson: "Clap Your Hands," "Hands on Shoulders," and "The Turtle" from *Let's Do Fingerplays,* by Marian Grayson. Reprinted by permission of Robert E. Luce, Inc.

Woody Guthrie: "Put Your Finger in the Air," words and music by Woody Guthrie. TRO- © Copyright 1954 (renewed), 1963 (renewed) Folkways Music Publishers, Inc. Reprinted by permission.

Maria Leach: "The Yellow Ribbon" from *The Rainbow Book of American Folk Tales and Legends,* by Maria Leach, copyright ©1958 by Maria Leach; "Transportation Problem" from *Noodles, Nitwits & Numskulls,* by Maria Leach, copyright © 1961 by Maria Leach. Reprinted by permission of HarperCollins Publishers, Inc.

Bascom Lamar Lundsford and Lamar Stringfield: "I Wish I Was a Mole in the Ground" from *Thirty and One Folk Songs from the Southern Mountains,* by Bascom Lamar Lunsford and Lamar Stringfield. Copyright 1929 by Carl Fischer, Inc., New York. Copyright renewed. Reprinted by permission of Carl Fischer.

Allan Miller and Marie Winn: "John Jacob Jingleheimer Schmidt" from *Fireside Book of Songs,* by Allan Miller and Marie Winn. Copyright © 1966 by Allan Miller and Marie Winn. Reprinted by permission of Simon & Schuster, Inc.

Margaret E. Mulac: "The Busy Farmer's Wife," "The Shopping Trip," "The Lion Hunt," and "One Finger Keep Moving" from *Fun and Games,* by Margaret E. Mulac. Copyright © 1956 by Margaret E. Mulac. Reprinted by permission of HarperCollins Publishers, Inc.

Ogden Nash: Excerpt from "The Adventures of Isabel" from *The Bad Parents' Garden of Verse,* by Ogden Nash. Copyright 1936 by Ogden Nash. Reprinted by permission of Little, Brown and Company and Curtis Brown, Ltd.

Iona and Peter Opie: "The Dark House" and "Silly Riddle" from *The Lore and Language of Schoolchildren,* by Iona and Peter Opie, 1959. Reprinted by permission of The Clarendon Press, Oxford.

Cook F. Potter: "The rat ran over the ridge of the roof . . ." from *More Tongue Tanglers and a Rigamorole,* by Cook F. Potter. Reprinted by permission of HarperCollins Publishers, Inc.

Ennis Rees: "Rhyming Riddles" from *Riddles, Riddles Everywhere,* by Ennis Rees. Copyright © 1964 by Ennis Rees. Reprinted by permission of the author.

Laura E. Richards: "Antonio," by Laura E. Richards, from *Child Life* magazine. Copyright 1935, 1963 by Rand McNally & Company. Reprinted by permission of John Richards and Rand McNally & Company.

William Jay Smith: "The Toaster" from *Laughing Time,* by William Jay Smith. Copyright © 1955 by William Jay Smith. Reprinted by permission of Harriet Wasserman Literary Agency, Inc.